YOU'RE IN
BUSINESS!

GET A JOB

AT A BUSINESS

Ryan Jacobson

Illustrations by Jon Cannell

Lerner Publications Company • Minneapolis

For Karla and Chris, who helped me get my first
job at a business (as a waiter) —R.J.

To Roland Young—You changed the way I looked at
things and left a lasting impression long after I
graduated from Art Center. Thank you. —J.C.

Lerner Publications Company
A division of Lerner Publishing Group, Inc.
241 First Avenue North
Minneapolis, MN 55401 USA

For reading levels and more information, look up this title
at www.lernerbooks.com.

Library of Congress Cataloging-in-Publication Data

Jacobson, Ryan.
    Get a job at a business / by Ryan Jacobson ; illustrated
by Jon Cannell
      pages   cm. — (You're in business!)
    Includes index.
    ISBN 978-1-4677-3838-5 (lib. bdg. : alk. paper)
    ISBN 978-1-4677-4755-4 (eBook)
    1. Teenagers—Employment—Juvenile literature. 2. Job
hunting—Juvenile literature. 3. Employment interviewing—
Juvenile literature. I. Cannell, Jon, illustrator. II. Title.
HD6270.J33 2015
650.14—dc23   2013046648

Manufactured in the United States of America
1 - CG - 7/15/14

TABLE OF CONTENTS

INTRODUCTION:

GET HIRED NOW!

You need money, right? You want to buy things. But maybe you've heard that you can't get a job. No one will hire you. You're too young.

If you think you need to be sixteen or older to find work, think again. Many jobs are available to people as young as fourteen. When you're old enough, one of them could be yours.

Of course, jobs come with rules. You'll need a work permit before you can start. You'll also need permission from a parent or

a guardian. There are limits to the amount of time you can work per day and per week—especially during the school year. But if you follow those rules, you'll be able to start earning money.

Even so, landing a job won't be easy. You might be competing against older students for the same positions. But by developing your skills and by taking a smart approach to job hunting, you'll give yourself a great chance for success!

FAST-FOOD ATTENDANT

Quick! You want a job that's fun and keeps you busy. But you've never worked before, so you have no experience. How will you get hired?

One answer: turn to the fast-food industry. Fast-food restaurants offer plenty of entry-level positions. These jobs don't require any previous experience. So once you turn fourteen, you can get hired as a fast-food attendant.

First off, become familiar with the options in your area. Become an occasional customer at the place where you hope to work. If you don't enjoy eating fast food, pick up a snack for a friend or a family member. Go inside to order. Get to know the menu. Learn the prices. Make a good impression with every visit. When the time comes to apply, maybe the manager will recognize you.

You can also help your chances by gaining related experience. Look for volunteering opportunities elsewhere in food service. Help serve meals at an area homeless shelter, at your place of worship, or at school or community events. Work on your customer service skills: listening carefully, responding politely, and working quickly but carefully.

Jobs at many fast-food restaurants open up on a regular basis. So you're welcome to apply at any time. Many of the restaurants' websites list available positions. Some also offer online applications and even provide interview tips. If possible, pick up your applications in person at each restaurant. Dress as if you're going to a job interview. You just might be. At some places, you may be interviewed as soon as you apply. If not, you still want to make a good first impression. Ask to see the manager in charge of hiring. Introduce yourself to him or her, and say how much you'd like to work there. This one-on-one contact could go a long way toward getting you hired. If you don't get interviewed on the spot, you may get called in at a later date. (Check out page 36 for tips on nailing a job interview!)

If all goes smoothly, you'll find yourself working as a fast-food attendant. The job title isn't very specific—and with good reason. Sooner or later (depending on age restrictions), you'll be doing all sorts of tasks. One day, you may be in charge of cleaning. That includes taking care of the bathrooms, emptying garbage cans, and wiping down tables. The next day, you may be behind the counter putting together sandwiches or in the kitchen cleaning vegetables. You could be asked to wash dishes or to stock supplies. Eventually, you may learn to take customer orders and to run the cash register. You may even get to staff the drive-through window.

All that variety means you'll have an opportunity to learn a lot of different job skills. And that'll come in handy a few years down the road. Someday, you may decide to apply for a promotion or for a job at a different company. And when you do, you'll be ready!

Working Wisdom: Work Permits

A work permit is a legal document that grants you permission to work. In most states, you'll need one before starting a new job. (Some states require it for people under sixteen. Others require it for anyone under eighteen. Either way, that's you!) Visit your school counselor to find out who issues permits for your school district. Your school's staff may be able to give you a copy of the form you need to fill out. Or you can check your state's labor department website to find the form online. Bring the form to the person who issues permits. You'll need to provide proof of your age, such as your birth certificate. Then a work permit will be created for you.

Your employer must fill out part of the form, listing your job duties and hours to be worked. When the employer is finished, the form goes back to where you got it. As soon as it gets approved, you're free to work at that job.

BUSSER/ DISHWASHER

Do you like the idea of working in food service but don't want to come home smelling like french fries? Sit-down restaurants have opportunities too. Most commonly, you can get hired as a dishwasher or a busser. These two jobs often go hand in hand. You may get a position that includes both sets of duties, or you may find work doing just one or the other.

As a dishwasher, you'll be in the kitchen area, behind the scenes. Most restaurants have high-powered dishwashing machines that do the washing for you. But you'll need to scrape extra food off plates and rinse all the dishes. Then you'll move everything into the machine. You'll also put the dishes away once they're clean.

It might sound like a snap, but working as a dishwasher can get pretty frantic. During the busy hours, a stream of dirty dishes can pile up in your

area. Your coworkers will be counting on you to get those dishes ready for the next round. If you stay focused, you'll have the satisfaction of watching that stack shrink.

Like dishwashing, bussing is simple but active. After a group of customers leaves, the busser clears the table and takes the dishes to the dishwashing area. Carrying a large stack of dishes can be a fun challenge. But on the flip side, it can be embarrassing to drop those dishes in front of a room full of people. (Not to mention that your boss won't be happy!) So a busser needs to have good judgment as well as good balance.

If you've got your eye on a restaurant job, it's helpful if you and your family are familiar customers. But it's okay if you're not. You can check out a restaurant's website to learn about the menu, prices, and atmosphere. Then gain experience by volunteering. Start at home by cleaning the dinner table and washing the dishes. Your family will be thrilled! From there, help out with meals at a homeless shelter or lend a hand with food-related fund-raisers, such as bake sales.

To start your job hunt, check the local newspaper and restaurant websites for openings. The restaurants themselves might also post Help Wanted signs. But even if you don't find any job advertisements, it doesn't hurt to apply. Stop in to pick up an application or drop off a résumé. It's important to look your best and be specific about which job you hope to get.

Once you land a position, remember that you don't have to bus tables or wash dishes forever. One benefit of working in a restaurant is that there's room to advance. By starting a job now, you have time to get promoted before you finish high school. If you prove to be a great employee, you can move up the ranks to take on hosting duties or even join the waitstaff.

Working Wisdom:
An Application Education

Every job application is different. Some can only be completed online. Others have to be filled out by hand. But if you're prepared, you can ace anything a company throws at you.

First, gather the information you'll need. This includes addresses and dates where you've volunteered, plus contact details for people who've agreed to be your references—adults who can recommend you for a position. If you pick up an application in person, bring this info with you. A business may expect you to fill out an application on-site. So be ready, just in case. But if you can bring the application home, do it. That way you won't feel rushed to finish it, and you can make corrections more easily.

Either way, take your time. Read the instructions. Answer every question. (If a question doesn't apply to you, write "not applicable.") If you're writing your answers by hand, print neatly. Then proofread to make sure you didn't make any mistakes. When you're sure the application is flawless, you're ready to turn it in.

GROCERY BAGGER

Everybody needs groceries. And most people buy them at local grocery stores. Those busy stores need workers. If you're organized and quick on your feet, grocery bagging could be a great job for you.

Of course, some large grocery stores don't use baggers. The customers bag their own groceries. But if you've ever been to a supermarket that does employ baggers, then you've probably seen them in action. They're the folks who put all the groceries into bags, and they move pretty fast. They also help customers bring groceries to their cars.

Maybe you and your family chat with your grocery baggers as they work. That's another clue to what this job has in store. Bagging groceries is especially fun if you enjoy being around people. You'll interact with coworkers, who may include classmates and friends. And you'll get to know plenty of people who live in your community. After all, many of them pass through the store at least once a week.

Want to give it a shot? First, do some volunteering to learn the skills you'll need. Many communities have food shelves, or food banks, run by volunteers. You can help sort donated food. You can stock the food on tables and shelves. And you can pack boxes of food for individuals and families. That kind of sounds like bagging groceries, doesn't it?

To really stand out, help coordinate a food drive. Figure out what kinds of food your food shelf especially needs. Then set up a place and time for people to bring these foods to your school, community center, or other accessible location. Advertise the event with flyers, a notice in the local paper, or postings on community websites and social media. After the drive, pack up the donated food and bring it to the food shelf. This kind of project shows you're organized, motivated, and reliable. (And transporting all that food will give you plenty of bagging experience!)

Put these activities on your résumé, and start filling out applications at nearby grocery stores. You might get interviewed on the spot. But chances are you'll get called for an interview at a later date. Along with a job interview, some employers require applicants to take a few tests. You may need to show that you have basic math skills. You may also take a personality test. For the most part, personality tests simply aim to check that you're honest and hardworking. But some questions might be about your preferred work style. (Do you like to work alone or with others? Are you good at following instructions? How do you react when something goes wrong?)

Don't sweat it. You can't fail a personality test. If the test shows that your personality doesn't fit the company, you probably wouldn't like working there anyway. On the other hand, if you're the kind of person this business tends to hire, you'll likely enjoy the job and get along with your coworkers.

Fast-forward. You've been hired. Are you ready for the challenges of grocery bagging? The job isn't always as simple as it seems. You'll need to ask customers what kinds of bags they want—paper, plastic, or their own reusable bags. Then you'll have to pack those bags carefully based on how strong they are and how much they can hold. If a shopper buys a lot of heavy items, such as milk cartons or canned foods, those items may need to be spread out over different bags instead of crammed into a single bag. Breakables, such as eggs, and squishy items, such as bananas or bread, go on top. You should ask customers if they want their raw meats bagged separately. Ditto with cleaning supplies. And all of this has to happen while other customers wait in line for their turn.

Once a customer's groceries are loaded up, you may need to offer a hand with the next step. Shoppers often need someone to bring bags out to their cars. In some stores, it's company policy for a bagger to do this unless a customer says not to. At other places, a bagger only provides the extra service when a customer asks. One way or another, you'll probably find yourself pushing a cart across a parking lot fairly often. That goes for the hottest, coldest, and rainiest days of the year!

On the upside, you get to be active and meet a lot of new people. If you're friendly to customers, the time will pass quickly. And your arm muscles will soon be in top shape!

Working Wisdom:
Writing a Résumé

Some job seekers are afraid of the word *résumé*. It sounds like a fancy, official document. But anyone can write a résumé. Just take it one step at a time.

First, search online for sample résumés. Choose a style that you like, and model yours after it. Your contact information goes on top. Follow that with your work experience, including odd jobs such as babysitting or lawn mowing. Add your volunteer work. Then list your education (your school and GPA) and any extra activities you're involved in. If you still have room, finish by listing your hobbies and interests.

Before you're done, proofread your résumé. Have someone else, such as a parent or a teacher, proofread it too. Then print as many copies as you need. (For an extra professional touch, use résumé paper, which you can get from an office supply store.)

A grocery-bagging position offers plenty of opportunities for promotion. As you get older, you can move into a higher-paying role, such as stocker or cashier. Or you can slide into a specialized job in the bakery or the deli. But meanwhile, make the most of your grocery-bagging gig. Enjoy the company, the action, and the possibilities!

MOVIE THEATER EMPLOYEE

What makes a job truly great? It's not just the paycheck. It's the whole package—the people, the place, and the perks. That's why so many young workers dream of getting hired at a movie theater. The environment can be fast-paced and exciting sometimes, yet relaxed and low-key at others. On top of that, movie theater workers are often treated to popcorn, soft drinks, and other snacks. Plus they have a chance to see movies for free!

If this sounds like the job for you, you're not alone. So you'll need to separate yourself from the competition. The best way to do this is through volunteer work. Choose volunteering opportunities that fit your interests. If you enjoy interacting with others, spend time at a nursing home. If you like to be in charge, organize a fund-raiser, such as a lemonade stand. Later, list your volunteer activities on your applications. Line up some references too.

With a strong application and a solid interview, you may soon be working at a movie theater. Your main duty will be cleaning the rooms where the movies are shown. This needs to be done before the theater opens. It also happens in between movies, after one audience leaves and before the next enters.

If you're good with people, you may also find yourself working as a ticket taker. In this role, you'll check people's tickets before they enter. Depending on the size of the theater, you may also give directions.

As you gain more experience, you could work at a concession stand. This may mean making popcorn and filling cups of soft drinks. Eventually, you'll also learn to take customer orders and operate a cash register.

No matter what your task, your mission is to give moviegoers a pleasant experience. Always try to be polite and friendly, even if customers are rude to you. Someone might be upset if a movie showing is sold out or if the line for the popcorn is especially long. Apologize for any inconvenience, but don't let one patron stop you from serving others. Alert a supervisor if a customer is disruptive.

Your work environment may vary depending on the time of year, the hours you work, and how many hot movies are playing in the theater. You'll have some whirlwind shifts when the rush of customers doesn't seem to stop. At those times, you'll need to work quickly without getting careless. Other days might crawl by with hardly any

business. Those are opportunities too. Ask your supervisor for extra tasks, make friends with your coworkers, and find other ways to pass the time in a fun but productive way.

As for perks, your employer will explain the rules. Not all theaters offer freebies to their workers. At places that do, there are limits to when and how much you can cash in on your employee privileges. For instance, don't expect to watch any free movies during your shift. If it's allowed, you can come back and catch a show when you're not scheduled to work. If you give the job your best effort, those privileges will be well-deserved!

Working Wisdom: Who's Your Reference?

Many job applications require you to list two or more references. The people you volunteer for are prime candidates. You can also consider teachers, family friends, and neighbors. Ask your top choices if they're willing to be references for you. If they agree, make sure you have their contact information. Employers will want to get in touch with them to find out if you're someone they can count on. Each time you list someone as a reference on an application, give that person a heads-up. That way he or she will know to expect a call soon.

OFFICE ASSISTANT

Where do you see yourself in fifteen years? Do you dream of working in an office setting? You might be able to get a foot in the door a lot sooner than you thought! Starting at the age of fourteen, you can gain valuable experience by working as a part-time office assistant.

Many businesses need someone to do basic clerical work: filing, managing mailings, and data entry. The job isn't for everybody. You'll be in a professional environment. That means dressing nicely every day and keeping yourself well groomed. It also means a lot of quiet time working on your own. Tasks can be repetitive. And you probably won't work with any people your own age. If you're okay with that, this position can be rewarding. And the skills you'll learn will help you for many years to come.

Your first step is to prepare a résumé. Be sure to mention any social media expertise you have. Social media is still relatively new. Many businesses are way behind on using it. If you know your way around sites like Facebook, Twitter, and Google+, list those skills on your résumé. If social media isn't your forte, no worries. Chances are you know how to use common computer programs—and even some not-so-common ones. Any software you're familiar with is well worth including on a résumé.

Tech savvy comes in handy, but what a desk job really requires is someone who's focused, organized, and efficient. How do you show these qualities on a piece of paper? By padding your résumé with volunteer work. Maybe your place of worship needs someone to photocopy bulletins. Perhaps a local nonprofit wants help folding letters and stuffing them into envelopes. You can also look for opportunities through your school. Are you involved in student government or in any clubs? Run for secretary. Taking notes during meetings and keeping that information organized will prepare you for bigger responsibilities. Does your school have a newspaper? Join the staff. You'll hone your typing skills and become an expert at meeting deadlines.

Once you've got a strong résumé, look for job postings in the local newspaper. Have a trusted adult help check online ads. Ask neighbors and family friends if their companies are looking for office help. When you get some leads, stop by specific businesses to ask about possible openings. On these visits, take along a parent or a guardian—plus copies of your résumé, just in case. With persistence and luck, you may land an interview and a small square of office space!

You might be hired to help your employers master social media. In that case, you may work one-on-one with people at the company. You'll take them through the step-by-step processes of using apps or websites. You might set up company accounts on these websites. And you might help maintain those accounts,

posting updates or photos on a regular basis.

More likely, you'll spend a lot of time photocopying documents, organizing files, and typing information into a database. You'll be asked to shred old documents, type handwritten meeting notes, and stuff envelopes. You may empty office garbage cans and pick up recycling from people's desks. Approach every task—even the boring stuff—with enthusiasm. Do the work thoroughly. When you finish a project, ask for another.

As you do your job well, you might be given more responsibility. You could start running errands, such as picking up supplies or delivering important documents. Sure, you're not old enough to drive, but if you know your way around the area and carry a cell phone in case of emergencies, you can go on foot, by bike, or by public transit. Eventually you might also be asked to help answer telephones. A calm, positive, and polite attitude will mark you as a prime candidate for this responsibility.

Aim to learn as much about the company as you can. Make a point of remembering people's names. Know their job titles and where their desks are. Let them know you're there to help if they need you. If something needs doing, people are likely to think of you. And down the road, when you're ready to move on to a different job, you can count on getting some sincere letters of recommendation. Plus you'll have plenty of unique and useful experience to add to your résumé. From there, the sky's the limit!

Working Wisdom: More than a Job Description

When businesses hire new employees, they're not just looking for job skills. They want to know what kind of person you are. Friendly? Reliable? Hardworking? Make sure your application answers all those questions with a resounding yes.

Do you participate in extracurricular activities such as sports, drama, or band? That tells employers a lot about you. You're social. You're a team player. And you work hard. Volunteering also gives you a leg up—even if it's unrelated to the job you want. It shows you're willing to put in extra effort for something that matters to you. Getting good grades will help too. That proves you can pay attention, solve problems, and get the results you need. If you're both successful in the classroom and active outside of it, employers will see that you can balance different commitments. They'll view you as someone who will take a job seriously and handle responsibility well.

RETAIL WORKER

Have you ever walked into a store, ready to spend your hard-earned money, only to realize you needed help? Maybe you didn't know where the video game section was. Or you loved those jeans but couldn't find a pair in your size. Or you needed to swap an earlier purchase for something better. Someone—a store employee— stepped up to give you a hand. But someday soon, the tables could be turned. You could be the helpful employee instead of the needy customer.

Retail is a little word that can have a huge variety of meanings. The place where you bought your fall clothes? That's retail. The sporting goods outlet where you got new gear? That's retail. Bookshops, pet supply stores, garden centers, electronics stores? You guessed it: retail. Any store that sells products directly to customers falls into this category.

That means your job opportunities are limitless, right? Not quite. While it's legal for fourteen-year-olds to work at most retail jobs, each store has its own policy. So your first step is to check out all the retail outlets in your area and find out which ones will accept your application.

If you come up with a fairly sizable list, you can narrow it down further. Think about your interests. Are you into sports? Fashion? Reading? Crafts? Do any of the retail stores on your list sell things that you like? Maybe you're even a regular customer at a few of them. Move those places to the top of the list.

Then start your pre-application training. Scout out your top choices. Browse their selections. Get familiar with their layouts. Notice how employees dress. Some places issue uniforms. Others expect employees to wear appropriate clothing of a particular color or style. Listen carefully to how employees talk. They've probably memorized a script for how to greet customers. Keep all this in mind. That way you'll have a pretty good idea of what to expect if you get hired.

After you've done your scoping, go ahead and apply. On your application—and in your interview—mention any activities and interests that connect to the store's mission. If you apply to a garden center, you might note the time you spend helping out in a neighbor's garden. If you want to work at a pet store, describe your pet-sitting experience. Above all, be positive

and enthusiastic. A good attitude goes a long way in retail.

Once you're hired, your supervisor may give you a variety of tasks. As a new employee, you'll likely work behind the scenes, without much customer interaction. But you'll have a chance to move out front when you prove you're ready.

You'll start with simple jobs. You may sweep floors—especially if you work at a place that tends to get messy, such as a garden center. You may unpack boxes of new merchandise and restock the shelves. (If you've got a good eye for decorating, you may get to arrange a display.) Or you may be in charge of keeping shelves organized. Customers often move things and knock stuff over. It's up to the employees to keep everything looking tidy.

Speaking of customers, they're your top priority. Get used to greeting them cheerfully and answering their questions. That's where your knowledge of the store's layout and inventory will come in handy. After all, the most common question you'll hear is, "Where can I find . . .?"

You may also get questions about the specifics of a certain item, so work on mastering the details of each product in the store. It may take a long time to master all that information. But once you do, you'll become a very valuable employee!

Early on, your assignments may be less than thrilling. But keep a positive attitude and work hard. You'll impress your bosses and snag a different role in no time. Handling the cash register or seeking out customers in need of assistance will keep boredom at bay. Whatever your role, you'll be able to create positive shopping experiences for others—and earn some cash for the next time you want to be a customer.

THEME PARK
WORKER

When you think of work, do roller coasters, cotton candy, and games come to mind? They may if you're looking for work at a theme park. For many people fourteen or older, this isn't just a dream job. It's a reality!

But wait. Before you start picturing yourself at Disneyland, remember that it's impossible to get hired at a major theme park without loads of experience. Instead, think about the regional theme parks near you. These are the ones that everyone in your area knows about. But people on the other end of the country probably never heard of them. If you hope to someday work at a nationally known park, you'll need to put in a few years at a regional one. And even if you don't ever plan to move to Anaheim or Orlando, you'll still have a rewarding experience as a theme park worker.

First, though, you've got some planning to do. How close is the nearest regional theme park? How will you get there if you're hired? Can you use public transportation, or will you need a lift from a family member or other trusted adult? What times of the year is the park open? If it operates year-round or at least during parts of the school year, figure out what days and times you can work. (Keep in mind that by federal law, people under sixteen aren't allowed to start a work shift after seven in the evening during the school year.)

Once you've figured out those details, you can start looking for specific job listings. Check park websites. Even if no openings are posted yet, you can get familiar with the positions that are usually available. And you can find out each park's minimum hiring age. (Fourteen is the legal minimum, but some parks have higher age requirements.)

Regional theme parks offer a wide range of jobs. Of course, you're too young for some of them, such as operating rides. But that still leaves you with plenty of possibilities. For instance, you could work at a concession stand (which is a lot like fast food, so see that section for tips.) Many theme parks have pools, so lifeguard positions may be open. You could also work at the front gate, greeting guests and checking their tickets.

Then there's the job of game attendant. Many consider it to be the most fun position available. You get to master a game, so you can show guests how to play it. Then you can cheer them on and hand out prizes if they win (which doesn't happen often). If dart throwing or ringtosses appeal to you, look no further for the perfect gig.

Most theme parks have mascots walking around. Of course, they're just employees dressed in hot, heavy costumes. If you can handle the discomfort, that's an interesting job too. You get to walk around the park, high-fiving kids, posing for pictures, and clowning around—and getting paid for it!

Some theme parks will want you to apply through their websites or via e-mail. Others may let you turn in an application on-site. One way or another, your application needs to show that you'll be a valuable employee. List volunteer opportunities that prove you're good with people, especially children. If you've ever been a babysitter, you're in good shape. Do you help out at a local day care? Are you a mentor or a tutor? Those kinds of activities will give you an edge.

You're even more likely to get hired if you have first-aid training. Classes are sometimes offered through community education, community centers, and hospitals. And if you're a certified lifeguard,

Working Wisdom:
Have a Transportation Plan

If you're lucky, your place of work will be close to
home. But you'll still need a plan for getting there and
back. If it's within walking distance, does a parent or a
guardian consider the route safe? In that case, carry a
cell phone and tell your family your work schedule, so
that they know when to expect you home. The same goes
for taking public transportation. Otherwise, arrange
for a family member or a trusted adult to give you
rides. And come up with a way to thank your driver
for the help. Do a favor, make a gift, or use some
of your earnings to chip in for gas.

put that on your application too. It
shows you're a good person to have
around if someone gets hurt.

When you get an interview,
you want the company to see that
you're energetic and outgoing. This
is especially true if you're applying
for a job that puts you in front of
customers. If you seem like someone
whom guests will enjoy, the park will
have yet another reason to hire you.
If all goes well, you'll land a job that
could be the thrill of a lifetime!

LIFEGUARD

You've probably heard adults say that having a job is a big responsibility. But few jobs come with more responsibility than a lifeguarding position. As a lifeguard, your mission is to keep swimmers safe, mainly by helping them avoid dangerous situations. This means making sure everyone follows the rules. If the need arises, you may have to rescue someone who's in danger of drowning.

Some people become lifeguards for the wrong reason. They want to sit in the sun all day and work on their tans—or nap in style at an indoor facility. But in reality, lifeguarding is far from relaxing. A good lifeguard needs to be alert, observant, and able to react quickly in an emergency. Does that sound like you? Then get ready to dive in.

To be a lifeguard, you must be at least fifteen years old. You need to be a strong swimmer with a knack for staying focused. And last but not least, you have to get certified through a lifeguard training course. The course may be offered through the place where you want to work. It may also be available at other facilities with swimming pools, such as a high school or a community center, or at a beach if there's one in your area. The course will include CPR and basic rescue skills.

Any place where people swim is a potential job site for you. Community pools and local beaches frequently hire lifeguards. But you may also find work at hotels, apartment buildings, senior centers, or high schools. Some state parks and summer camps hire lifeguards too.

To figure out how to apply, start by researching online. Learn what you can from facilities' websites, and follow any application instructions provided. If websites don't give you much information, take a more direct approach. Visit each place and talk to someone in charge. Look for a manager or a head lifeguard—someone who supervises other lifeguards.

Once you start the application process, you'll need to provide proof that you're a certified lifeguard. So bring your certification card when you pick up and drop off applications. And most important, bring it to job interviews.

During an interview, you won't need to get in the water and pass any swimming tests. Your certification already proves that you can. So dress nicely and expect a normal question-and-answer session. If you get hired, your employers may decide to retrain you. But don't worry. It doesn't mean they think you're not good enough. It's probably just their company policy.

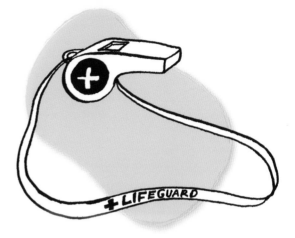

With the training under your belt, you'll be off to a good start. You probably won't be the only lifeguard on duty during your shifts. Other lifeguards may be stationed around the facility or along the beach. A head lifeguard will likely supervise you and assign you a spot to work.

You'll stand or sit alone, and you'll observe. Your job is to see everything. The best lifeguards are the ones who don't get distracted. They don't enter conversations, and they don't let themselves daydream. They concentrate on their important work.

You must constantly watch for possible danger. If anyone is breaking safety rules, you'll have to put a stop to the dangerous behavior. That means you must be able to speak up and take charge. Be polite but firm. Make it clear that swimmers need to follow your instructions. If someone ignores you, you can tell that person to get out of the water and leave. Alert the head lifeguard if someone is being especially difficult.

The most important part of your job will also be the most stressful. If someone is struggling in the water, you'll need to act fast. You might not always be sure if someone needs saving. But "better safe than sorry" is a wise policy for a lifeguard. If you overreact, you can always apologize. And as you gain more experience, your instincts will improve.

From time to time, if there are more than enough lifeguards on duty, your supervisor may give you non-guarding tasks. You may add chemicals to the pool, help with cleaning, or even sell concessions.

These jobs will give you a chance to move around, chat with others, and relax a bit. Just make sure you follow instructions carefully. And be ready to jump back into guard mode at a moment's notice.

With training, discipline, and a positive attitude, you could have the makings of a first-rate lifeguard. Someday your abilities may save a person's life. And they'll serve you well at any other job you have down the road.

PARTING WORDS

Even though you may not be sixteen yet, there's a lot you can offer an employer. If you're dedicated, dependable, and ready to make the best of any situation, businesses will want you on the payroll. And if you begin building your skills and experience now, you may turn your first job into the springboard for a future career. So start working on those applications! You'll be hired in no time.

If you're ready to start earning money, begin with an action plan. Grab a sheet of paper or hop onto a computer. Then answer the questions below:

What skills do you have? How will you get the training and experience you need? What volunteer opportunities will help you build job skills? Do you have a work permit?

How much time can you spend working? Do you have other commitments that may interfere? How many hours do you want to work per week? Check the Department of Labor's rules to find out how much you're allowed to work. It depends on the time of year.

What kind of help will you need from adults, including your family? Who will be your references? How will you get to and from work? Can anyone point you to possible job opportunities?

How will you find job opportunities in your area? Which nearby businesses hire people under sixteen? Do they have websites where you can learn more? If you visit a business, whom can you talk to about applying for a job?

NAIL THAT INTERVIEW!

If you've been called in for a job interview, your application probably impressed someone. But that doesn't automatically mean you'll get hired. Several people may be interviewing for the position. And only one will be chosen. Follow these interview tips, and that lucky new employee could be you!

1. **Do your homework**. Before an interview, research the company you hope to work for. Learn about its history and mission. Study the job description for the position you want. Write down questions to ask your interviewer. (You should always ask at least one or two questions of your own during an interview. This shows you care about the job and have thought about the details.)

2. **Practice interviewing.** You can find sample interview questions online. Rehearse your answers alone by talking to a mirror. Notice your facial expressions. Try to look alert, calm, and upbeat as you speak. Then take it to the next level. Have a relative, a friend, or a teacher interview you. That way, you can practice your answers in front of a live audience.

3. **Dress for success.** You don't need to show up in a fancy dress or a suit. But make sure your clothes are clean and in good condition. Consider what your outfit says about you. For instance, a T-shirt with a vulgar message or logo won't win you any points. On the other hand, an unwrinkled dress shirt or tasteful sweater with black pants will say you're taking the interview seriously.

4. **Make a strong first impression.** Arrive for the interview slightly early. Seven to ten minutes ahead of time is perfect. (More than that is overkill.) Shake hands firmly. And remember to smile!

5. **Be your best self.** Maintain a positive attitude. Answer questions honestly— even if that means saying, "I don't know." Focus on your ability to learn new skills quickly and your willingness to work hard.

6. **Say thank you.** At the end of the interview, thank your interviewer for his or her time. Later that day, send a handwritten thank-you note.

7. **Follow up.** Before you head home, ask your interviewer when you can expect to hear back about the job. If you don't get a call within that time, go ahead and contact your interviewer. Thank him or her again for the interview and say that you're just checking in to see when a decision will be made.

GLOSSARY

certified: declared fit and able to perform a task after receiving training and passing a test. To be a lifeguard, you'll need to get certified.

clerical: related to office work. Clerical tasks can include stuffing envelopes and updating databases.

entry-level: not needing any previous experience. Most jobs available to students your age are entry-level positions.

perk: something extra that a person receives for doing a job. A perk of working at a theme park is that you get to ride the rides for free.

personality test: a questionnaire designed to reveal what kind of person you are. Some jobs require you to take a personality test before getting hired.

promote: to move an employee to a more important position in the company. You may get promoted after working somewhere for a few months or years.

proofread: to check a document for errors and make corrections. You should proofread applications before turning them in.

reference: a person who agrees to speak with potential employers about you and the work that you do. When you do volunteer work, ask a person you're volunteering for to be a reference.

retail: the business of selling products in small quantities to customers for their own use. A cosmetics store and a sporting goods store are both retail stores.

waitstaff: the group of servers at a restaurant

work permit: a legal document that grants you permission to work. If you're under sixteen, you will need a work permit before starting a new job.

FURTHER INFORMATION

Donovan, Sandy. *Job Smarts: How to Find Work or Start a Business, Manage Earnings, and More*. Minneapolis: Twenty-First Century Books, 2012. Read about how to find and succeed in the right kind of job for you.

Fradin, Dennis B., and Judith Bloom Fradin. *Earning.* New York: Benchmark, 2011. This book offers an introduction to working and using your paycheck well.

Harmon, Daniel E. *First Job Smarts.* New York: Rosen Publishing, 2010. Learn how to prepare yourself for starting your first job.

My First Resume
https://www.careerkids.com/resumeSSL.php
This site features a form you can fill out and use as a starting point in creating your résumé.

TeensHealth: 5 Ways to Ace a Job Interview
http://kidshealth.org/teen/school_jobs/jobs/tips_interview.html
Read tips on how to be successful at a job interview.

YouthRules!
http://www.youthrules.dol.gov
Learn the legal limits and rules for getting a job before you're sixteen, know your rights as a worker, and see the work stories of other people your age!

PHOTO ACKNOWLEDGMENTS

The images in this book are used with the permission of: © Alex Varlakov/Hemera/Thinkstock, pp. 2, 4, 19, 22 (Post-its); © Adam Alaoui/ iStock/Thinkstock, pp. 2, 4, 20, 21, 22 (paper clips); © Imageman/ Shutterstock.com, pp. 2, 27, 28, 29 (cotton candy); © graphicnoi/iStock/ Thinkstock, pp. 3, 16, 17 (popcorn); © severija/iStock/Thinkstock, pp. 4, 5, 9, 10 (bubbles); © coprid/Shutterstock.com, p. 4 (dishes and soap); © flyfloor/iStock/Thinkstock, pp. 5, 12, 13, 15 (groceries); © Michael Aubry/iStock/Thinkstock, p. 5 (burger); © baibaz/istock/Thinkstock, p. 6 (shake); © artemisphoto/Shutterstock.com, p. 6 (fries); © iStockphoto. com/karandaev, p. 9 (cups and saucers) © iSailorr/iStock/Thinkstock, pp. 12, 14 (peppers); © bhofack2/iStock/Thinkstock, p. 16 (licorice); © LUHUANFENG/iStock/Thinkstock, p. 18 (seats); © moodboard/ Thinkstock, p. 20 (pens); © ULKASTUDIO/Shutterstock.com, p. 23 (jeans); © Todd Strand/Independent Picture Service, pp. 23, 24, 25 (money); © serezniy/iStock/Thinkstock, p. 24 (T-shirt); © moodboard/ Thinkstock, p. 26 (pillows); © iStockphoto.com/lucato, p. 26 (price tag); © iStockphoto.com/kreicher, p. 28 (ticket stand); © chevanon/ Shutterstock.com, p. 30 (dart); © Konstantin Faraktinov/Shutterstock. com, p. 31 (sunscreen); © studioVin/Shutterstock.com, p. 31 (sunglasses); © OSORIOartist/Shutterstock.com, p. 34 (life preserver); © iStockphoto. com/pepifoto, pp. 32, 34 (sand).

Front Cover: © argus/Shutterstock.com (ticket); © OSORIOartist/ Shutterstock.com (life preserver); © M. Unal Ozmen/Shutterstock.com (ice cream); © R. Gino Santa Maria/Shutterstock.com (groceries).

Main body text set in Avenir LT Std 11/18.
Typeface provided by Adobe Systems.